369 Manifestation Journal

Daily Journaling to Manifest Abundance, Love, Wealth, Emotional Well-being, and Your Heart's Desire

© Copyright 2025 - All rights reserved.

The content contained within this book may not be reproduced, duplicated, or transmitted without direct written permission from the author or the publisher.

Under no circumstances will any blame or legal responsibility be held against the publisher or author for any damages, reparation, or monetary loss due to the information contained within this book, either directly or indirectly.

Legal Notice:

This book is copyright-protected. It is only for personal use. You cannot amend, distribute, sell, use, quote, or paraphrase any part of the content within this book without the consent of the author or publisher.

Disclaimer Notice:

Please note the information contained within this document is for educational and entertainment purposes only. All effort has been executed to present accurate, up-to-date, reliable, and complete information. No warranties of any kind are declared or implied. Readers acknowledge that the author is not engaging in the rendering of legal, financial, medical, or professional advice. The content within this book has been derived from various sources. Please consult a licensed professional before attempting any techniques outlined in this book.

By reading this document, the reader agrees that under no circumstances is the author responsible for any losses, direct or indirect, that are incurred as a result of the use of the information contained within this document, including, but not limited to, errors, omissions, or inaccuracies.

Your Free Gift
(only available for a limited time)

Thanks for getting this book! If you want to learn more about various spirituality topics, then join Mari Silva's community and get a free guided meditation MP3 for awakening your third eye. This guided meditation mp3 is designed to open and strengthen ones third eye so you can experience a higher state of consciousness. Simply visit the link below the image to get started.

https://spiritualityspot.com/meditation

Or, Scan the QR code!

Table of Contents

INTRODUCTION 1
START YOUR 369 PRACTICE..2
SECTION 1: BEGIN 3
ATTRACT ABUNDANCE DAILY 10
SECTION 2: ABUNDANCE..11
INVITE LOVE INTO YOUR LIFE..19
SECTION 3: LOVE 20
FUEL FINANCIAL SUCCESS 31
SECTION 4: WEALTH 32
MANIFEST INNER PEACE 42
SECTION 5: EMOTIONAL WELL-BEING 43
CONCLUSION 51
HERE'S ANOTHER BOOK BY MARI SILVA THAT YOU MIGHT LIKE......53
YOUR FREE GIFT (ONLY AVAILABLE FOR A LIMITED TIME) 54
REFERENCES..55
IMAGE SOURCES 58

Introduction

Manifestation can help you align your energy and mindset with your goals to live the life you have always wanted. The 369 Method is one of the most popular and effective manifestation strategies. It focuses on practicing affirmations, intentions, and other techniques in a specific sequence to help you achieve your goals.

The book begins by introducing the 369 Method and explains how it can help you manifest your desires. It then describes how you can attract abundance with daily good habits that can transform your life. You will also learn to harness the power of manifestation to invite romantic love and self-love into your life.

The 369 Method can put you on the path to financial success and help you achieve your financial goals. You will also discover the power of intention and learn how it can help you gain clarity and focus your energy on manifestation.

The last chapter focuses on manifesting emotional well-being and inner peace to cultivate a clear and positive mindset. The book includes various exercises and daily rituals that reinforce your manifestation journey. Creating a consistent mindful practice that aligns your thoughts with your goals is key to manifesting your desires.

Your dreams are just a few affirmations away. Begin your journey today and transform your life.

Start Your 369 Practice

Section 1: BEGIN

Life is meaningless without dreams. Every person has some kind of goal they want to reach. Some want to find love, while others want to buy a big house or get a promotion. While some goals are easy to achieve, others can be challenging. Manifestation can bridge the gap between dreams and achievement. However, manifestation isn't a magical solution to all your problems. It is a method that can transform your mindset by replacing negative thoughts with positive ones.

Using the 369 method is an effective manifestation tool.[1]

The 369 technique is one of the most popular and effective manifestation methods to help you attract your desires. This chapter introduces the method and provides exercises and prompts to help you to manifest your dreams.

The 369 Method

The 369 Method is a manifestation tool for focusing thoughts, bringing intentions to life, and laying the groundwork for future manifestation success. It involves writing your goal three times in the morning, six times in the afternoon, and nine times in the evening. The repetition of this sequence can amplify your intention as you send it out to the universe and align its vibrations with your goals. It also shifts your mindset. Repeating affirmations strengthens your self-confidence, replaces negative thoughts with positive ones, and helps you to develop a successful mindset. The 369 Method includes affirmation, visualization, journaling, and setting intention.

Consistency is key when practicing the 369 Method because it creates a rhythm that aligns with the universe's energy and reinforces your intention in your subconscious mind. Writing your manifestations multiple times makes it a sacred ritual that creates a strong frequency of expectation and belief. Going days without manifestation can disrupt your focus and energy flow.

The method is based on Nikola Tesla's theory that the numbers three, six, and nine are powerful and hold the key to the universe. The numbers also hold significance in the law of attraction and numerology making it one of the most powerful manifestation methods available.

- **Number Three:** This represents manifestation, self-expression, creativity, and your connection with the divine. It also symbolizes the link between the spirit, the mind, and the body.
- **Number Six:** It is associated with harmony, balance, stability, and inner strength. The number can increase your spiritual power and align your energy with that of the universe.
- **Number Nine:** It symbolizes transformation, rebirth, new beginnings, and letting go of the past.

The 369 Technique has gained popularity recently due to its simplicity and power. It does not require much work. You just set an intention for what you want to manifest, creating affirmations in the present tense that align with your desire, such as *"I am grateful for the love that fills my life."* Repeat the affirmation using the 369 Technique and visualize your life as if your dreams have already been manifested.

While manifestation is a powerful tool, it will not work without action. Work hard, take advantage of opportunities, and believe in yourself. Aligning your intention with your actions can strengthen your manifestation.

Prompts and Exercises

These exercises will start you on your manifestation journey. Work on them in the order they are presented below.

1. Write Your Manifestation Statement

Create a clear, concise manifestation statement that reflects your primary goal. The statement must be in the present tense, as though the desire has already been realized. Example: *"I am grateful for attracting abundance into my life."* Write and/or recite this statement three times in the morning, six times at midday, and nine times before bed, following the 369 Method.

_____

_____

Visualization Exercise

Close your eyes and vividly visualize that you have already achieved your goal. Focus on sensory details – what you see, hear, feel, and experience. Make your visualization realistic by including every detail and engaging your five senses. For instance, imagine the colors of the trees, leaves, and flowers if you visualize a forest. Watch the birds in the trees and animals running at a distance. Smell the flowers around you, feel the cool breeze on your skin, and listen to the birds singing and the leaves crushing under your feet. After you have finished, write down what you experienced. If you do not know what to write, these questions can help you.

- Describe everything you saw and everyone you encountered.

_____

_____

_____

- Write down all the sounds you heard.
  _____
  _____
  _____

- What did you feel throughout the visualization?
  _____
  _____
  _____

- Did a person or an animal speak to you? What did they say?
  _____
  _____
  _____

- Did you see something unusual?
  _____
  _____
  _____

- Was there a message from the universe in the visualization? What was it?
  _____
  _____
  _____

- Would you repeat the experience? Why or why not?
  _____
  _____
  _____

2. Create a Daily Ritual for 369 Practice

Set specific times during the day to perform your 369 practices (morning, midday, and night). You should create a calming ritual to accompany your writing, such as lighting a candle, practicing mindful breathing, or meditating for a few minutes. Perform your 369 practices consistently at the same times each day.

Calming Breathing Exercise Instructions:
1. Find a quiet room with no distractions.
2. Lie down or sit in a comfortable position.
3. Close or open your eyes. Choose whatever makes you comfortable.
4. Place one hand on your belly and another on your chest.
5. Take a long, deep breath through your nostrils. Feel the air fill your lungs as your stomach rises below your hands.
6. Breathe out through your mouth and feel your belly fall under your hand. Notice how the hand over your chest does not move as much.
7. Repeat three or four times while focusing on your belly's movement.

Calming Meditation Instructions:
1. Find a quiet room with no distractions.
2. Sit in a comfortable position with your back straight.
3. Breathe at your normal pace.
4. Close your eyes and only focus on your breathing.
5. Feel the air as it enters through your nostrils and fills your body.
6. Notice how the air exits your body through your mouth.
7. You may experience distracting thoughts while meditating. Do not focus on them, resist them, or allow them to distract you.
8. Acknowledge these thoughts without judgment, let them pass, and bring your attention back to your breathing.

3. Gratitude Practice for Manifestation

Practice gratitude before manifestation to boost your mood, reduce stress, and remind yourself of all your blessings. This will help you focus on the good things in your life and put you in the right frame of mind to manifest. When you are focused on the positive, you will believe that more good things can happen to you, reinforcing your intention.

Make it a habit to write in your journal every day about three things you are grateful for, such as your home, family, friends, career, etc. You can also write about small things that happen to you, such as having a good cup of coffee or receiving a loving message from an old friend.

4. Affirmations
- I am grateful for the small steps I take every day.
- I find joy every day.
- I let go of negative thoughts and replace them with positive ones.
- My thoughts are peaceful and calm.
- I treat myself with respect, patience, and kindness.
- I attract positivity wherever I go.
- I am excited about the opportunities I attract.
- I am grateful for my skills and abilities.
- My joy comes from within.
- I find the bright side in every situation.
- I embrace happiness.
- My past does not control my decisions.
- I only allow healthy relationships in my life.
- I manifest joy every day.
- I celebrate my achievements every day.
- I choose to bring joy to others every day.
- I prioritize my health and happiness.
- External factors do not determine my worth.
- I chase passions and interests that make me happy and fulfilled.
- I manifest the life I want.
- I trust my inner voice.
- I make choices that bring me closer to my heart's desire.

5. Check-In Section
Track your manifestation progress by writing down how many times you have manifested.

The 369 Method is a powerful manifestation technique that can alter your mindset to focus on the positives. It aligns your thoughts and energy with your goals to motivate you to take action to make your dreams a reality. Practice manifestation using the 369 sequence daily to remain consistent and attract your heart's desire.

Attract Abundance Daily

Section 2: ABUNDANCE

The 369 Method can help you attract abundance. Affirmations and other manifestation techniques can align your thoughts and actions with an abundance mindset, promoting positive energy, prosperity, and good habits.

Learn how the 369 method can help you attract abundance.'

This chapter explains the concept of abundance and its impact on your daily life. It also explores the importance of gratitude and affirmations.

Abundance

Abundance is the belief that there is enough success, happiness, and wealth for everyone. Life is filled with opportunities. If one door closes, another will open. This mindset encourages you to be optimistic and to approach life's challenges with a positive attitude. Say you apply for a job and get rejected. Instead of feeling angry or defeated, consider that this was not the right job for you and that a better one will soon come along.

People with an abundance mindset see opportunities instead of challenges. They believe that even the hardest experiences can have positive outcomes. They know there is a lesson, better options, or a chance for growth behind every rejection or break-up. This mindset also encourages them to focus on the positive and appreciate the good things in their lives instead of obsessing over what they do not have. They learn to embrace every opportunity, accept that change is a part of life, and are unafraid to step out of their comfort zone.

Gratitude

Gratitude can alter your mood and transform your daily life. It shifts your attitude and thoughts away from negativity to a positive mindset. You start focusing on the good things in life and overlook the negatives. For instance, you are moving to a new apartment but cannot afford to hire a moving company. Instead of focusing on your money problems, you can focus on how fortunate you are to have a place of your own or siblings or close friends to help you move.

Practicing gratitude releases dopamine and serotonin, which improve your mood. It also reduces stress and anxiety.

The Importance of Gratitude

- **Increases Your Patience:** Expressing gratitude daily can reduce your impulsiveness, boost your self-control, and increase your patience.
- **Helps You Focus on the Positives:** Life can be full of distractions, and it is easy to forget all your blessings. You can also become fixated on the negatives during tough situations. However, practicing gratitude reminds you of all the amazing things in your life, no matter how hard things become. Writing down what you are grateful for will rewire your brain to always look for positive things.

- **Reduces Comparisons:** Practicing gratitude reduces negative self-talk and boosts your self-esteem. As a result, you will not feel the need to compare your life to the lives of others. You will be so happy and satisfied with your life that you will not pay much attention to what you lack.
- **Encourages Mindfulness:** People who practice gratitude do not think about past regrets or worry about the future. They simply focus on the present and appreciate what is happening in their lives. For instance, you have an important meeting next week, but today, you are meeting your best friend for coffee. Instead of worrying about the meeting, you are grateful for spending time with a friend and enjoying a nice drink.
- **Reminds You of What Matters:** When a person loses their job, they may feel that it is the end of the world. However, gratitude reminds you of what matters, such as your health, family, and having great friends. You will always find something to be thankful for, no matter how bad the situation is.

Affirmations

Affirmations are short, positive, and powerful statements that you repeat to yourself to replace negative thoughts with positive ones. These words tap into your subconscious to alter your mindset, challenge you, and motivate you to chase your goals.

The Importance of Affirmations

- **Reduces Stress and Boosts Confidence:** Affirmations build resilience and reduce stress. Repeating positive statements cultivates a positive attitude and makes you stronger. Phrases such as "I am strong and resilient and can handle anything life throws at me" or "I am capable of handling stress" can help you believe in yourself and handle challenging situations.
- **Increases Your Self-Esteem:** Affirmations reinforce positive beliefs about yourself. They challenge negative thoughts, counteract insecurity and self-doubt, and increase confidence. Statements such as "I believe in my abilities" or "I treat myself with kindness and respect" can shift your self-perception and encourage you to believe in yourself.
- **Boosts Your Mood:** Affirmations challenge negative thoughts and reduce stress, improving your mood and life satisfaction.

Gratitude and affirmations alter your mindset and help you focus on the positives. A positive mindset is necessary for setting intentions and for manifestation. You should be confident and optimistic and believe your dreams will become a reality.

Repeating affirmations every day can help instill a routine that aligns your mental focus with abundance.

Prompts and Exercises

1. Daily Gratitude Affirmations

Write down daily affirmations like, "*I am grateful for the abundance flowing into my life each day,*" and "*Every moment, I am surrounded by opportunities for prosperity.*" Write/recite these affirmations based on the 369 Method.

1. _____
2. _____
3. _____
4. _____
5. _____
6. _____
7. _____
8. _____
9. _____
10. _____

2. Visualization of Abundance

What does abundance mean to you? Close your eyes and visualize your life filled with abundance. Focus on sensory details – what you see, feel, hear, and experience in moments of prosperity. After visualizing, journal what you envisioned and repeat your chosen affirmation sequence according to the 369 Method.

_____
_____
_____

3. Create an Abundance Board

Create a physical or digital vision board that represents your abundance-related goals. This can include images, words, or symbols that resonate with your desires. Take a few moments three times daily to review the board and recite your affirmations six times, then reflect on how these visuals align with their daily practice.

4. Morning Journaling Pages for Abundance

Cultivate an abundance mindset by writing in your journal every morning things you are grateful for or happy thoughts to start your day on a positive note. These prompts will get you started if you do not know what to write.

- Write down three things you would like to manifest today and mention why.

- What three things can you do to increase your abundance today?

- Write down one goal you would like to achieve today.

- Set an intention for the day.

- What small change can you make today to help increase your sense of abundance?

- Write down what you want more of in your life, such as happiness, love, money, or success.
  _____
  _____
  _____

5. Evening Reflection

Write positive thoughts in your journal before bed to reflect on your day or what you want to achieve in the future.

- What are you grateful for today?
  _____
  _____
  _____

- Mention the people in your life you are grateful for.
  _____
  _____
  _____

- What did you love about yourself today?
  _____
  _____
  _____

- What went well into your life today?
  _____
  _____
  _____

- Mention five things you would do if money was not an issue.
  _____
  _____
  _____

- What makes you feel happy and fulfilled? What can you do to increase those moments in your life?
  _____
  _____
  _____

- Mention something that has affected you today.

  _____
  _____
  _____

- What would you like to manifest in the near future and why?

  _____
  _____
  _____

- What limiting beliefs do you have about abundance that may be holding you back?

  _____
  _____
  _____

6. Write a Letter

Write a letter to your future self to express your gratitude for the abundance mindset you have developed. Describe how you have changed and grown throughout the years – thanks to the abundance you have attracted.

_____
_____
_____
_____
_____
_____
_____
_____
_____
_____
_____
_____

7. Magical Powers

Close your eyes and imagine you have magical powers that you can use to cultivate abundance in one area of your life. Which area would you choose? How would you use your new mindset to improve your life?

_____
_____
_____

8. Limiting Beliefs

Write down three limiting beliefs that prevent you from cultivating an abundant mindset. How do they impact your life? How can you use the 369 Method to challenge these beliefs?

_____
_____
_____

Practice gratitude and affirmations using the 369 Method to attract abundance. Don't allow adversity to discourage you. Believe that opportunities are limitless and that life is filled with second chances. When something does not work out, believe that the universe has a better plan for you, and another opportunity will soon arise.

Invite Love into Your Life

Section 3: LOVE

Everyone is looking for love. They are either seeking romantic love and dreaming of finding their perfect partner, looking within, and trying to cultivate a healthy relationship with themselves, or wanting to nurture their bond with their friends and families. It is human nature to need to connect with others and develop healthy relationships. The 369 Method can help you manifest love through affirmations, meditations, and other exercises.

This chapter explores the connection between self-love, positive energy, and attracting external love. It also highlights the importance of aligning your thoughts and emotions to welcome love into your life.

The Connection Between Self-Love, Positive Energy, and Attracting External Love

Imagine you see two people walking down the street. One is confident, smiling, and radiating positive energy, while the other is frowning, lacking self-esteem, and radiating negativity. Which one would you approach? Most people will find the first person more likable and approachable because they gravitate toward confidence and positivity. Self-love and a positive attitude make you into a magnet for love.

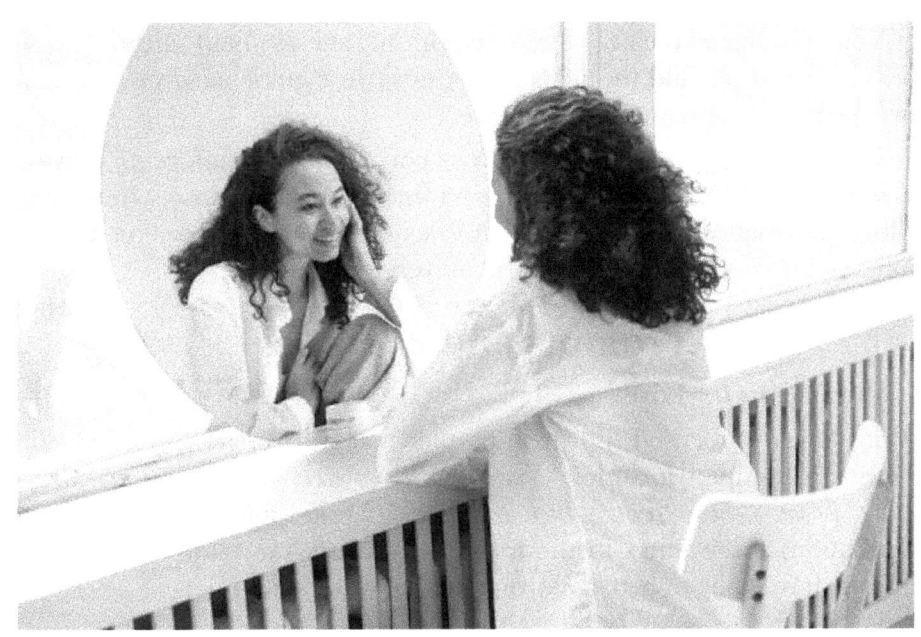
Manifestation starts with self-love.*

When you love and accept yourself, you attract positive emotions. People will see your self-love and radiant energy shining outward. You will become a secure, confident, and happy person who knows their worth. These characteristics will help you attract healthy relationships with like-minded individuals.

What you feel inward is reflected outward. You will not attract love if you do not believe that you deserve to be happy or see yourself in a negative light. You will only attract unhealthy relationships with people who do not respect you or treat you in the right way.

Importance of Aligning Your Thoughts and Emotions with Your Goal

Aligning your emotions and thoughts with your goal will motivate you to take action and commit to it. Your energy will be focused on finding love and welcoming it into your life. According to the law of attraction, your thoughts shape your reality. Your beliefs will put you on the right path. For instance, if you believe that you are worthy of love, you will start dating and looking for a healthy relationship. You will not tolerate disrespect or toxic individuals who do not treat you the way you deserve to be treated.

Your thoughts create vibrations or an energy field around you. Positive emotions and thoughts attract positive experiences, such as self-love, romantic love, and platonic love.

The 369 Method focuses on consistency, reinforcing loving intentions, and maintaining a vibration that draws love closer. Repeating a love affirmation following the 369 sequence keeps this emotion in mind and opens you up to what the universe has in store.

Prompts and Exercises

1. Affirmations for Love

Write ten love-focused affirmations that you will repeat using the 369 Method. Examples include: *"I am worthy of deep, unconditional love"* and *"Love flows freely into my life."* Write and/or recite these affirmations three times in the morning, six times at midday, and nine times before going to bed, following the 369 Method.

1. _____
2. _____
3. _____
4. _____
5. _____
6. _____
7. _____
8. _____
9. _____
10. _____

2. Gratitude Practice for Love

Make it a daily habit to write down three things you are grateful for in your relationships or yourself. This will help foster a loving mindset and align your energy with attracting love.

_____
_____
_____

3. Daily Loving-Kindness Ritual

Create a daily self-care ritual, such as a moment of reflection or a loving-kindness mantra. Examples include, *"May I be loved, may I be at peace, may I share love with others."* Repeat this mantra following the 369 pattern, building a sense of inner love.

4. Heart-Opening Visualization

Instructions:

1. Find a quiet room with no distractions.
2. Sit in a comfortable position.
3. Take a long, deep breath, hold it for a few seconds, and exhale with a sigh, emptying all the air in your lungs.
4. Feel your feet grounded by having your feet flat on the ground.
5. Imagine the energy in your heart waking like a cat from its slumber.
6. Visualize your heart waking up in the present.
7. Imagine a golden tube of light flowing out of your heart and moving through your body, leaving a light trail in its path.
8. After the light flows throughout your body, watch it as it slowly and gently exits and disappears into the Earth.
9. You feel your heart and mind relaxing as you watch the light traveling to the Earth's center.
10. You see a crystal-shaped light glowing and radiating peaceful energy from the Earth.
11. It makes you feel calm, centered, and peaceful.
12. It draws your energy to it like a magnet. You watch the golden tube emerge from the Earth, merge with the crystal-shaped light, and become one.
13. You watch both energies together while you breathe slowly. You feel as if time stands still.
14. Take a deep breath of gratitude and feel the energy enveloping you.
15. It is quiet and peaceful. The energy moves slowly through your legs and flows throughout your whole body.
16. You are filled with the Earth's energy now.

17. Breathe slowly and feel yourself sinking into your heart's space.
18. Connect with your heart and set an intention. What does your heart tell you? What does it need to know?
19. Now, feel the combined energy filling it with light.
20. Your heart is bright, golden, and shines like a diamond.
21. The light fills it with grace and love.
22. Visualize the energy flowing through you. Your heart can't contain the energy anymore. It wants to escape.
23. Take a deep breath and open the gates of your heart. You can feel the energy beaming out, shining through you, and spreading like wildfire.
24. As you watch the energy spreading, you see beacons of light shining at a distance. It is the energy of all your loved ones.
25. You see your energy merging with theirs. All the energies are now one and shining brighter than ever before.
26. Your heart is now open to love and inviting others to connect with it. You are ready to love unconditionally.

5. Round-up Journaling Questions

Reflect on your emotional state by answering these journal questions.

- How have you shown love to yourself this week?

  _____
  _____
  _____

- What new loving experiences have happened this week?

  _____
  _____
  _____

- What does your heart need?

  _____
  _____
  _____

- How can you treat yourself with kindness and compassion?

- How can you express yourself authentically?

- Are you at peace with yourself? If not, why not?

- How can you lead a happier life?

- Do you have healthy relationships? If not, what can you do about it?

- Do you need to work harder on your relationships? If yes, what should you do?

- Where do you find inspiration?

- How do you stand up for yourself?

- How can you forgive yourself?

- How can you forgive others?

- Are your thoughts positive or negative?

- How can you strengthen your spiritual connection?

- Do you say "yes" when you should be saying "no"?

- Are there feelings you are holding back?

- What do your spirit, mind, and body need?

- What is your biggest accomplishment?

- Mention five things you love about yourself.

- What makes you different from others?

- Name three flaws you accept about yourself.

- What is standing in the way of loving yourself?

- Why do you believe you deserve happiness?

- What can you do now that your future self will thank you for?
  _____
  _____
  _____

- Mention three things you need to do to practice self-care.
  _____
  _____
  _____

- Write down five things people usually say about you.
  _____
  _____
  _____
  _____
  _____
  _____

- What makes you feel alive?
  _____
  _____
  _____

- What labels do you use to describe yourself?
  _____
  _____
  _____

- When was the last time you did something nice for someone? What did you do? How did it make you feel?
  _____
  _____
  _____

- Write a thank you letter to yourself.

___

- What makes you happy?

___

- What would you want to do with your life if money was not an issue?

___

- What makes you feel loved?

___

- Mention three things you love about your body.
  _____
  _____
  _____

- What destructive habits do you want to quit?
  _____
  _____
  _____

- How do you cheer yourself up when you have a bad day?
  _____
  _____
  _____

- Who is your support system? How do they make you feel?
  _____
  _____
  _____

- When was the last time you overcame a challenge? How did you overcome it?
  _____
  _____
  _____

- What does your ideal day look like?
  _____
  _____
  _____

6. Love Check-In log

Log your love manifestation progress in a calendar.

Love is the most beautiful gift that you give to yourself and others. Practice manifestation exercises every day to attract love into your life.

Fuel Financial Success

Section 4: WEALTH

Who does not want to be wealthy? Some people believe that financial success can be challenging. While inflation makes life hard, you can still find ways to save money and improve your financial situation. To do that, you must let go of the limiting beliefs holding you back and embrace a healthy mindset that drives you to act. Manifestation can change your mindset. It will help you to improve your relationship with money, change your spending habits, and make better financial decisions.

Fuel your financial success using the 369 method.'

This chapter helps you attract and sustain financial success with consistent practices that align your mindset and energy with your financial goals.

How Mindset, Beliefs, and Visualization Practices Impact Financial Success

Your mindset is directly linked to your financial success. It can either hold you back or push you towards working harder and succeeding. It can also influence your financial decisions and spending habits. A negative mindset will weigh you down and prevent you from taking action, which can negatively impact your relationship with money. As a result, you will struggle with saving and may end up with a huge debt. On the other hand, a positive mindset will be focused on abundance. It will motivate you to pursue your financial goals and manage your money wisely to build your wealth.

Some people have negative beliefs about money, such as the belief that money cannot buy happiness, money is the root of all evil, and you will never be able to save enough money to achieve your goals. These beliefs can prevent you from achieving financial success. However, if you self-reflect, you will realize that these beliefs stem from poor financial habits such as overspending or turning down investment opportunities. This realization can change your mindset and inspire you to change your financial behavior. For instance, you can repeat affirmations to challenge these beliefs, such as, "*I am in control of my spending habits*" or "*I save money to achieve my goals.*"

Visualization is another powerful tool for influencing financial success. Envisioning yourself rich and successful motivates you to act to make these images a reality. Visualization also changes your relationship with money. For instance, if you visualize yourself saving every month, you will start making better financial decisions, such as reducing expenses and setting money aside.

Repeating affirmations using the 369 sequence can help boost your confidence, keep you focused, and attract opportunities to achieve financial success. It will also change how you view money by replacing negative beliefs with positive ones.

You should also support a positive relationship with wealth and money. Your thoughts about money can affect your financial decisions and career choices. For instance, if you think you do not deserve to be rich, you will not ask for a raise at work nor make choices that can improve your financial status.

Many people believe they are not in control of their financial success. For instance, employees feel their bosses determine their salaries, and business owners find that their customers can either make or break their business. However, no one is in control of your financial situation but you. For instance, you can negotiate your salary or find ways to make your product more appealing.

Let go of the defeated mindset that makes you believe there is nothing you can do to be rich. Believe that money and wealth are not impossible to attain. Treat money as a means to help you achieve your goal instead of something that stresses you out or controls your life. Believe that you deserve to be wealthy and happy - and that money will make your life easier and better. Ignore thoughts like, "*Money can't buy happiness*," as these thoughts can prevent you from achieving your financial goals.

Money can make your life less stressful. If you have enough money, you will not worry about paying rent or supporting your family. You will be able to afford good healthcare and take time off from work when you need to relax and unwind. Once you see money as a tool to improve your life, you will work harder to succeed financially.

Prompts and Exercises

1. Financial Abundance Affirmations

Write daily financial affirmations using the 369 Method, three times in the morning, six at midday, and nine at night). Examples of affirmations: "*Money flows easily into my life*" and "*I am open to new financial opportunities.*"

1. _____
2. _____
3. _____
4. _____
5. _____
6. _____
7. _____

8. _____
9. _____
10. _____

2. Money Block Journaling

This exercise will help you reflect on your beliefs about money. Write responses three times throughout the day using the 369 Method.

- What do you believe about money?

  _____
  _____
  _____

- Are these beliefs helping or hindering you?

  _____
  _____
  _____

- How did your parents' relationship with money influence you?

  _____
  _____
  _____

- Have your limited beliefs about money held you back? What would you do differently if you had a second chance?

  _____
  _____
  _____

- Have societal beliefs about money influenced you?

  _____
  _____
  _____

- What advice would you give to your past self to change their beliefs about money?

  _____
  _____
  _____

- What lessons have you learned from the financial challenges you have faced throughout your life?

  _____
  _____
  _____

- What is your current financial mindset?

  _____
  _____
  _____

- Has your self-worth impacted your financial decisions?

  _____
  _____
  _____

- What beliefs do you have about money that have impacted your identity? (Examples, "I am bad with money" or "I will never be rich").

  _____
  _____
  _____

- How does money make you feel? How do these emotions impact your financial decisions and your relationship with money?

  _____
  _____
  _____

3. Visualization of Financial Success

Close your eyes and imagine a life where financial worries are a thing of the past. Make your visualization vivid by imagining every detail and engaging your five senses – what does your home look like? How do you feel about paying for things comfortably? Include any other sensory experiences. Afterward, write down key aspects of this visualization and repeat the 369 affirmation sequence.

_____
_____
_____

4. Mindful Spending Exercise

Dedicate a part of your day to mindful spending – reflecting on where you spend money and how it aligns with your financial goals. Answer prompts followed by the 369 affirmation practice.

- Does your spending align with your goals?

  _____
  _____
  _____

- What do you usually spend money on?

  _____
  _____
  _____

- Do you waste money or spend it wisely?

  _____
  _____
  _____

- Do you have a budget? Do you stick to it? If you don't, why not?

  _____
  _____
  _____

- When was the last time you bought something you did not need? How did that make you feel?

  _____
  _____
  _____

- Write down your expenses for the last week. What purchases were unnecessary? Is there something you can do without saving money?

  _____
  _____
  _____

5. Wealth Gratitude Journaling

Write down your financial accomplishments daily, big or small, or any steps you have taken that bring you closer to your goals. Express your gratitude for the smart decisions you make or all the resources you have that help you on your journey.

Examples

- I am grateful for my monthly salary, which allows me to take care of my expenses and save for emergencies.
- I am grateful that I do not spend my money on unnecessary things, which allows me to save and achieve my financial goals.
- I am grateful that I am starting to make smart financial decisions that change my relationship with money.
- I am grateful that I cook at home instead of wasting money on takeout.
- I am grateful that I buy my clothes during the sale and save money.

6. Daily Wealth Ritual

Create a personal daily wealth ritual tied to your 369 practice. For example, you could do deep breathing exercises, light a green or gold candle, or hold a coin while reciting your affirmations.

7. Financial Goal Setting Page

Prepare a financial plan that allows you to save money and make better financial decisions. First, you must study your expenses, recognize unnecessary spending, and make cuts to save money. You should also set a budget and make sure to stick to it. Add your other financial goals, such as how much money you want to save in a month or year, what you plan to do with the money, investment ideas, etc.

8. Round-up Questions

- Mention three financial goals you want to achieve today.

_____
_____
_____

- What can you do today to get closer to your financial goals?

  _____
  _____
  _____

- Mention three mindful exercises that can keep you aware of your spending habits and help you make smart financial decisions.

  _____
  _____
  _____

- What healthy daily habits do you practice that help you achieve your financial goals?

  _____
  _____
  _____

- What immediate actions can you take to improve your financial management skills?

  _____
  _____
  _____

- What can you do to become more disciplined with money?

  _____
  _____
  _____

- What knowledge do you need to become financially successful?

  _____
  _____
  _____

- Do the people in your life support your financial goals? What can you do to strengthen your relationship with them?

  _____
  _____
  _____

- What lessons have you learned from past experiences that can help you succeed financially?

  _____
  _____
  _____

- What opportunities are you planning to pursue to improve your finances?

  _____
  _____
  _____

- How will you overcome challenges that prevent you from becoming wealthy?

  _____
  _____
  _____

- How can you cultivate a positive mindset about money?

  _____
  _____
  _____

- How will you prioritize your needs to manage your expenses?

  _____
  _____
  _____

- How will you resist the temptation to avoid spending money on things you don't need?

  _____
  _____
  _____

- Mention advice you have received in the past that can help you achieve your financial goals.

  _____
  _____
  _____

- How will your life change when you achieve your financial goals?

    _____
    _____
    _____

9. Wealth Tracking Log

Track your expenses and savings to see your progress and how close you are to achieving your financial goals.

Do not let anyone tell you that you cannot dream. Success and wealth are possible. People achieve them every day. Believe in yourself, work hard, and manifest your goals to the universe. Change your relationship with money, make smart financial decisions, and make cuts to save money.

Understand that money is not evil or will not make you happy. It is a necessary tool to improve your life and provide you with the necessary resources to achieve your goals.

Manifest Inner Peace

Section 5:
EMOTIONAL WELL-BEING

Everyone wants to live a stress-free life without worrying about other people's opinions or letting daily issues get to them. However, life can sometimes be overwhelming, and you can struggle to stay calm. You may also blame yourself for every mistake or struggle to make peace with some aspects of your life.

A stress free life is what we all aim for.⁵

This chapter explores using the 369 Method to nurture emotional well-being and cultivate inner peace. Using the 369 Method as a daily anchor, you will discover how to align your mindset, promote self-compassion, and center your emotional state.

The Connection Between Emotional Wellness and Manifestation

Manifestation and emotional wellness are connected. Positive emotions and thoughts motivate you to act and achieve your goals. You will also feel empowered and believe in yourself, amplifying your intention and making your manifestation more effective. Manifestation, on the other hand, can improve your emotional wellness. It reduces stress and anxiety by bringing your attention to the positive aspects of your life and distances you from negative thoughts and emotions.

Emotional stability is essential for effective manifestation because it supports clear and positive thinking. Manifestation goes beyond repeating affirmations or visualizing the life you want to live. You should also believe in what you manifest, or it will not happen. For instance, two people repeat affirmations like, "*I deserve success and abundance,*" but one believes what they are saying, and the other does not. Which one do you think will take action to become successful? Emotional stability also keeps you in the right frame of mind to recognize the goals you want to manifest.

The 369 Method and manifestation can help you cultivate a peaceful mindset and enhance self-awareness. For instance, affirmations such as "*I am at peace with my past*" or "*I am smart and strong and can achieve my goals*" will help you cultivate a peaceful attitude and become aware of your strengths and abilities. Journaling and visualization can also keep you calm, reduce your stress, and help you to recognize your true power.

Prompts and Exercises

1. Affirmation Writing for Emotional Balance

Write affirmations promoting inner peace and emotional strength using the 369 Method (three times in the morning, six at midday, and nine at night), such as, "*I am grounded and at peace with myself*" and "*I choose calmness and positivity.*"

1. _____
2. _____
3. _____
4. _____
5. _____
6. _____
7. _____
8. _____
9. _____
10. _____

2. Self-Compassion Ritual

Create a personal self-compassion ritual tied to your 369 daily practice. For example, light a candle or place a hand on your heart while repeating, *"I am worthy of love and understanding,"* three times. Include notes on your experience.

_____
_____
_____

3. Guided Journaling on Releasing Negative Emotions

Answer these questions to identify and release emotional blocks.

- What emotions are you ready to release?

_____
_____
_____

- How do you feel after letting go of negative thoughts?

_____
_____
_____

- What triggered these emotions?

_____
_____
_____

- When was the last time you felt happy and safe? What can you do to feel this way again?

  _____
  _____
  _____

- How do you act when you experience negative emotions?

  _____
  _____
  _____

- What is your biggest fear?

  _____
  _____
  _____

- When was the last time you cried?

  _____
  _____
  _____

- How do you express and release negative emotions?

  _____
  _____
  _____

- What do you need to let go of to be happier?

  _____
  _____
  _____

- What can you do to prevent these emotional blocks?

  _____
  _____
  _____

4. Daily Inner Peace Meditation
Instructions:
1. Lie down or sit in a comfortable position.
2. Take a few deep breaths and clear your mind. Focus only on your breathing.
3. Close your eyes and focus on the air entering your nostrils and filling your lungs.
4. Feel the air as it is released through your mouth.
5. Notice how your chest and abdomen feel with every breath you take.
6. Bring your attention to your hands. Open your palms and feel the sensation in your fingertips and fingers.
7. Feel the vibrations from the energy of the universe fill your hands. Take a long, deep breath, and feel the vibrations flowing through your body, bringing you energy of peace.
8. Focus on the center of your forehead and open yourself to the white light of peace.
9. Let the white light wash over your body and fill you with healing energy. It heals every part of you.
10. It releases the tightness in your jaw, softens your eyes, releases the tension in your shoulders, relaxes your tongue and lips, relieves any pain in the abdomen and chest, and relaxes your entire body.
11. Take a deep breath and enjoy the inner peace you are feeling.
12. Focus on the present moment because it is all you have. You do not need to think about the past or worry about the future.
13. Feel completely at peace at this moment.
14. Imagine this peace spreading into every aspect of your life, including your job, relationships, and the places you frequent, such as your home.
15. When you lose touch with your inner peace, bring your awareness to the present moment.
16. Enjoy the quiet and feelings of stillness.

17. When you are ready, bring your attention back to your surroundings.
18. Notice the sounds around you, slowly open your eyes, and stretch your body.

5. Round-up questions

- Mention three things that bring you inner peace.

- What negative emotion, thought, or habit do you need to let go of to cultivate inner peace?

- How can you challenge thoughts that prevent inner peace?

- What calming and comforting words can you tell yourself now?

- What self-care activity can bring you inner peace?

- Does nature bring you inner peace? How?

- Do your relationships bring you inner peace? If not, what can you do to improve them?

  _____
  _____
  _____

- Does your job disturb your peace? If yes, what can you do to change your situation?

  _____
  _____
  _____

- What can you do to spread love and peace?

  _____
  _____
  _____

- What sounds or music make you feel calm and at peace?

  _____
  _____
  _____

- What has inner peace taught you about yourself and the world?

  _____
  _____
  _____

- What habits or physical activities help you cultivate inner peace?

  _____
  _____
  _____

- Which emotions are you trying to avoid? Why?

  _____
  _____
  _____

- What happens when you face these emotions?

  _____
  _____
  _____

- What do you need to cultivate emotional wellness?

  _____
  _____
  _____

6. Emotional Check-In/Tracking Log

Log your inner peace manifestation progress in a calendar.

Inner peace can reduce stress and provide the clarity needed to practice manifestation. Achieve emotional balance by practicing self-compassion and journaling. Remember, manifestation requires a positive mindset and emotions. Practice gratitude, focus on the good things in your life, and repeat affirmations that challenge negative thoughts and invite positive ones.

Conclusion

You can change your life with the power of the 369 Method. Affirmations, intentions, visualizations, and meditations can alter your thought pattern. They can motivate you to believe in yourself and work hard to achieve your goals because you know the universe is on your side. While there are many manifestation methods, the 369 Method has proven effective. It is also simple, and anyone can practice it, even those unfamiliar with manifestation.

The book explained the 369 Method and introduced practices such as visualizations, affirmations, and intentions. You discovered the impact of Tesla's powerful numbers on manifesting abundance with exercises such as gratitude, affirmations, visualization, abundance board, and journaling.

You learned to attract all types of love into your life to nurture long, healthy relationships with prompts and exercises such as loving-kindness rituals and love check-in logs. The 369 Method can also invite financial success into your life. You learned how to attract wealth with manifestation practices such as money block journaling, mindful spending exercise, and daily wealth rituals.

The last chapter focused on manifesting emotional well-being and inner peace with round-up questions and self-compassion rituals. All exercises in the book align your mindset with your desire to bring your dreams to life.

Consistency can amplify your manifestation. Make the 369 practices part of your daily routine to change your mindset and achieve your goals. This book can act as your guide. You can return to it whenever you need ideas on manifestation practices.

If you enjoyed this book, I'd greatly appreciate a review on Amazon because it helps me to create more books that people want. It would mean a lot to hear from you.

To leave a review:
1. Open your camera app.
2. Point your mobile device at the QR code.
3. The review page will appear in your web browser.

Thanks for your support!

Here's another book by Mari Silva that you might like

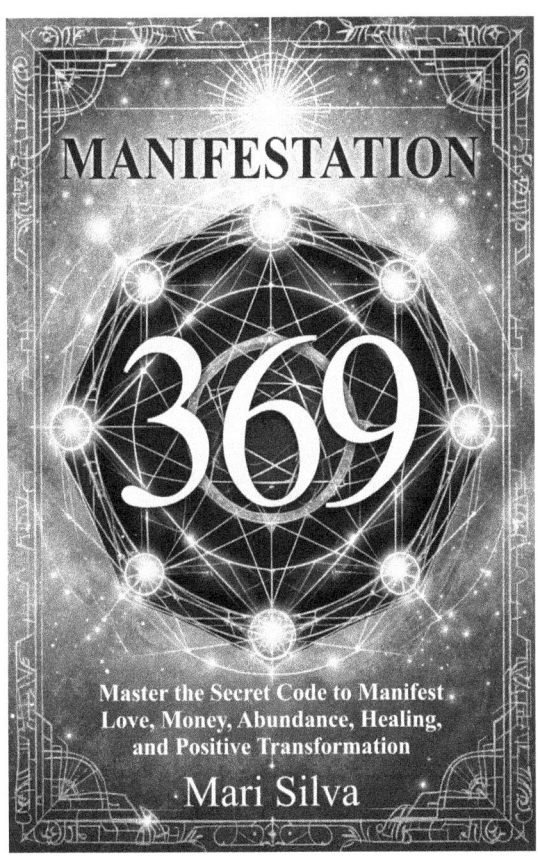

Your Free Gift
(only available for a limited time)

Thanks for getting this book! If you want to learn more about various spirituality topics, then join Mari Silva's community and get a free guided meditation MP3 for awakening your third eye. This guided meditation mp3 is designed to open and strengthen ones third eye so you can experience a higher state of consciousness. Simply visit the link below the image to get started.

https://spiritualityspot.com/meditation

Or, Scan the QR code!

References

Calm Blog. (2024, July 16). Calm Blog. https://www.calm.com/blog/369-manifestation-method

fcionline. (2019, December 16). 30 affirmations to power happiness and positive thinking. Fertility Centers of Illinois. https://www.fcionline.com/article/30-affirmations-to-power-happiness-and-positive-thinking/

Gupta, S. (n.d.). How to Manifest Your Goals With the 369 Method. Verywell Mind. https://www.verywellmind.com/manifest-your-goals-with-the-369-method-8620625

HowStuffWorks. (2024, October 1). Unlocking the Power of 3, 6, and 9: Exploring the 369 Manifestation Method. HowStuffWorks. https://science.howstuffworks.com/science-vs-myth/extrasensory-perceptions/369-method.htm

Marie, J. (2020, September 14). 23 Affirmations for Joy & Happiness - Janell Marie - Medium. Medium. https://janellmt.medium.com/23-affirmations-for-joy-happiness-d3042204007d

Mastering the 369 Manifestation Method to Achieve Your Dream Life - Centre of Excellence. (2024, February 23). Centreofexcellence.com. https://www.centreofexcellence.com/369-manifestation-method/

Neil, S. (2024, June 13). The 369 Manifestation Method: How-to and Success Tips | Mindset Motive. Mindset Motive. https://mindsetmotive.com/369-manifestation-method/#how-to-succeed-with-the-369-manifestation-method

Pyne, S. (2023, August 19). The 369 Manifestation Method: The power of number and steps. Hindustan Times.

https://www.hindustantimes.com/astrology/horoscope/the-369-manifestation-method-the-power-of-number-and-steps-101692420055127.html

Robinson, L., Segal, J., & Smith, M. (2018, October 23). Relaxation Techniques for Stress Relief - HelpGuide.org. HelpGuide.org. https://www.helpguide.org/mental-health/stress/relaxation-techniques-for-stress-relief

Michael, E. (2024, September 26). 120+ Daily Positive Mental Health Affirmations. MentalHealth.com. https://www.mentalhealth.com/tools/positive-mental-health-affirmations

Coach. (2024, February 21). ChantalG. Intuition. ChantalG. Intuition. https://www.chantalg.co.uk/journal-prompts/10-abundance-journal-prompts

Helfand, E. (2021, November 29). The Benefits of Positive Affirmations - Wellspring. Wellspring Center for Prevention. https://wellspringprevention.org/blog/the-benefits-of-positive-affirmations/

How to develop an abundance mindset: 8 tips to help you thrive. (n.d.). Calm Blog. https://www.calm.com/blog/abundance-mindset

Linsey. (2022, April 25). 30 Abundance Journal Prompts to Help You Manifest Your Dreams - Annais. Annais. https://annais.co.uk/abundance-journal-prompts/#google_vignette

Reid, S. (2022, June 6). Gratitude: The Benefits and How to Practice It - HelpGuide.org. HelpGuide.org. https://www.helpguide.org/mental-health/wellbeing/gratitude

Scantalides, A. (2022, January 19). 2 Evening Journal Prompts for a Positive & Abundant Mindset. Aligned & Empowered Coaching; Aligned & Empowered Coaching. https://ironbodybyartemis.com/2022/01/18/2-evening-journal-prompts-for-a-positive-abundant-mindset/

The power of gratitude: 6 benefits of a gratitude practice. (n.d.). Calm Blog. https://www.calm.com/blog/power-of-gratitude

Well-being, Y., & Youth, Y. (2021, July 2). The Importance of Affirmations. The Y. https://www.ymcansw.org.au/news-and-media/the-y-at-home/the-importance-of-affirmations/

Beachy, L. (2023, May). Law Of Attraction: Aligning Your Thoughts And Actions. Medium. https://medium.com/@lisabeachy/law-of-attraction-aligning-your-thoughts-and-actions-39b7c6223f33

Insight Network, Inc. (2024). Insight Timer - #1 Free Meditation App for Sleep, Relax & More. Insighttimer.com. https://insighttimer.com/murmurr_elixirs/guided-meditations/grounding-and-heart-opening-visualisation

Jenna. (n.d.). 25 Self-Love Journal Prompts. Musings from the Moon. https://musingsfromthemoon.com/blogs/blog/25-self-love-journal-prompts

monerin. (2016, December 23). Self-Love Attracts True Love and Leads to Greater Happiness. How to Be Happy. https://happinessblog.net/self-love-attracts-true-love-and-leads-to-greater-happiness/

Weingus, L. (2021, October 6). 60 Journaling Prompts for Self-Love. Silk + Sonder. https://www.silkandsonder.com/blogs/news/50-journaling-prompts-for-self-love?srsltid=AfmBOop4nHc--OER6_kxf5VcQ0HV8ow44TeRy6FsT6lSBAlBRfq4ZQrP

Houston, M. (2024, December 10). How To Build A Money Mindset For Financial Success In Business And Life. Forbes. https://www.forbes.com/sites/melissahouston/2024/12/10/how-to-build-a-money-mindset-for-financial-success-in-business-and-life/

Joseph, M. (2023, March 10). 52 Reflective Morning Journal Prompts for Inner Peace, Clarity, and Success. Thriving Good Life. https://thrivinggoodlife.com/morning-journal-prompts/

Lyons, Z. (2024, August 30). Mastering Money Mindset: How Your Beliefs Impact Your Financial Decisions. Coachingly.ai. https://www.coachingly.ai/blog/single/mastering-money-mindset-how-your-beliefs-impact-your-financial-decisions

Morrissey, M. (2023, November 9). 111 Journal Prompts for Money Mindset | Money Mindset Shifts 111 Journal Prompts for Money Mindset | Money Mindset Shifts. Brave Thinking Institute. https://www.bravethinkinginstitute.com/blog/life-transformation/journal-prompts-for-money-mindset

Munster, R. (2023, November 10). How Imagining Financial Freedom Can Shape Your Reality. Https://Www.moneyfit.org/. https://www.moneyfit.org/financial-visualization-success/

Hagen, P. (2024, August 21). 47 journal prompts for emotional awareness - Hagen Growth. Hagen Growth. https://hagengrowth.com/journal-prompts-for-emotional-awareness/

James, K. (2024). Insight Timer - #1 Free Meditation App for Sleep, Relax & More. Insighttimer.com. https://insighttimer.com/katejames/guided-meditations/inner-peace-meditation-9

Joseph, M. (2023, March 10). 52 Reflective Morning Journal Prompts for Inner Peace, Clarity, and Success. Thriving Good Life.com. https://thrivinggoodlife.com/morning-journal-prompts/

Pendergast, H. (2023, June). Does positive manifestation for mental well-being work? - Safety and Management Solutions. Safety and Management Solutions. https://www.samsltd.co.uk/does-positive-manifestation-for-mental-well-being-work/

Image Sources

1 https://www.pexels.com/photo/woman-in-black-top-sitting-on-brown-armchair-3331574/
2 https://www.pexels.com/photo/person-holding-fan-of-us-dollar-bills-4968655/
3 https://www.pexels.com/photo/sitting-blur-reflection-face-6417918/
4 https://www.pexels.com/photo/smiling-woman-in-fur-coat-posing-5922465/
5 https://www.pexels.com/photo/woman-spreading-both-her-arms-2529375/